THE ULTIMATE GUIDE TO TAX CREDITS FOR TECH COMPANIES

HOW TO BEGIN SAVING $221,000 A YEAR IN AS LITTLE AS 4 WEEKS

By JOE SKULSKI
Chief Savings Officer

THE ULTIMATE GUIDE TO TAX CREDITS FOR TECH COMPANIES

HOW TO BEGIN SAVING $221,000 A YEAR IN AS LITTLE AS 4 WEEKS

By JOE SKULSKI

TAX Credits For Tech Companies
http://www.taxcreditsfortechcompanies.com
Element56
23 Katelyn Lane
Lancaster, NY 14086
Joe@taxcreditsfortechcompanies.com
PHONE: (888) 913-5676

Cover and interior design by Andrea Wood Schmitz (http://industrythoughtleaders.com)

All rights reserved. No part of this book may be reproduced or transmitted in any form or by any means, electronic or mechanical, including photocopying, recording or by any information storage and retrieval system, without written permission from the authors, except for the inclusion of brief quotations in a review.

Limit of Liability Disclaimer: The information contained in this book is for information purposes only, and may not apply to your situation. The author, publisher, distributor and provider provide no warranty about the content or accuracy of content enclosed. Information provided is subjective. Keep this in mind when reviewing this publication.

Neither the Publisher nor Authors shall be liable for any loss of profit or any other commercial damages resulting from use of this guide. All links are for information purposes only and are not warranted for content, accuracy, or any other implied or explicit purpose.

Earnings Disclaimer: All income examples in this book are just that -- examples. They are not intended to represent or guarantee that everyone will achieve the same results. You understand that each individual's success will be determined by his or her desire, dedication, background, effort and motivation to work. There is no guarantee you will duplicate any of the results stated here. You recognize any business endeavor has inherent risk for loss of capital.

Copyright by Joe Skulski
ASIN: B00G3VN2QY
ISBN-13: 978-1493772827
ISBN-10: 1493772821

Published in the United States of America

Table Of Contents

Introduction	1
Why Am I Doing This?	5
Do You Know Your Government Wants You To Develop Innovative Products?	7
What is the Research and Development Tax Credit?	11
How much can we get?	13
Why Didn't Your Accountant Tell You About This?	15
How Do I Know If I Qualify?	19
Are We Too Small To Take Advantage Of This?	23
What Is The Right Process To Take The R & D Credits?	27
How Much Does The Research and Design Study Cost?	35
How To Get Started?	37
Final Thoughts	40
About The Author	41

Chapter 1

Introduction

"It's not how much money you make that matters, but how much you keep"
- Robert Kiyosaki

I have been in business for a while. I have run divisions of big global companies, lived overseas and worked on start-ups. I worked in food production, medical devices, technical service businesses and technology.

I am currently CEO of a technology company and I get excited about all the great things that come with running the company. The company is dynamic and there are so many opportunities and things to do: upcoming releases, speaking to customers, working with sales, designers, programmers, marketing and the content people. I do it for the pursuit of putting out the best software in our industry to meet the needs of our customers.

There is another side of being CEO of a tech company that is hard. It keeps me up at night as it probably does you. It is the business side. There is payroll to meet, late invoices to deal with, pitches for funding, communicating with shareholders and reporting financials to the board. I am quite sure that most technology executives did not get in this game for the love of this side of the business. This is the side that CEOs and founders have trouble getting their heads around and making time for. Some like it…..most don't.

I am one of those CEOs that likes getting into the game of saving money. I am a self-proclaimed "Chief Savings Officer". Don't get me wrong, I like to get sales and lots of them, but I like to save where I can. I am always on the lookout for ways to save: 1) where I don't have to do the work and 2) when it will have an immediate impact. I don't like hiring consultants to do multiple-year efficiency studies to ring out 1% here or .8% there. I don't like to allocate the use of paper clips or firing people to save a buck. I like savings that I can put on autopilot or where I can expend the least amount of resources for big payoffs. I like fast, easy, quick and big savings wins!

This book is about something that can immediately increase your profits. Profits get more programmers, more marketing people, more sales people or more money in your pocket. It is something that you can do today. I found out about it and learned that all the big guys like Apple, Dell and many others have been doing for years. They use it and you can too!

This thing that I discovered and use is something that every CEO needs to investigate. This thing is called Research and Development Tax Credits. I know that this will not get your creative juices flowing but it is something that you should know about and more importantly know how to get it done. It could mean hundreds of thousands of dollars or more to your bottom line.

Think about it this way, say you can save $300,000 to your bottom line and you have a profit margin of 10%. This is like an extra $3,000,000 in sales! And the savings are not a one-time thing. As long as there is the R&D Credit (remember the big guys don't want this going away) and you pursue them they can be a recurring source of increased cash flow for your company.

The Ultimate Guide to Tax Credits For Tech Companies

Chapter 2

Why Am I Doing This?

I've done it and I want to share it with you. Your government wants to create innovation. They want you to do it and are willing to help fund it. Nobody told me about this…not school, not my accountants, lawyers or the government. I want you to know about it and for you to put it in place in your business.

As I mentioned before I am all about finding the money! I enjoy it and advise companies on how to do it all the time. I know many ways to find hard-earned cash. I operate a business outside of my software CEO gig to consult with and deliver savings to companies.

I want to give you CEO perspective and approach. This book will not give you the in and outs of Tax Code (you would not read it if it did). You pay people for that. Maybe you have a great accountants and tax lawyers that do all this. But, if you are like many of us you don't have the type of people that put this in front of you. I'll give you an executive view, enough to make a decision if this is right for your company and give you the ROI that you want.

It is not hard as you may think and I want to show you how I did it and how painless it can be done right. Sure, my eyes roll back in my head when I first started to speak with some accountants about it, but I refined the process and now your company can do it painlessly, quickly and most importantly by someone other than you. You're too busy delivering great products!

Chapter 3

Do You Know Your Government Wants You To Develop Innovative Products?

"Innovation is the central issue to economic prosperity" - Michael Porter

Software development firms, Tech Companies, and Manufacturers that develop software or put out product have a hard enough time recruiting great programmers & engineers, keeping people trained on the latest software, hitting their release dates, dealing with bugs & patches and taking product to market.

One thing that keeps CTOs, CFOs and CEOs up at night is having to keep justifying the costs of their technical teams, figuring out how to raise money from investors or keeping their shareholders happy. They must always answer questions like: should we outsource?, do we need that many developers? why can't this be cheaper?

Companies that develop software should have a great strategy in their arsenal on how to minimize their development costs. Research and Development Tax Credits (R&D Credit) are a great way to drop money to the bottom line. The big guys like Google and Apple do this each and every year and a lot of small and medium sized business do not know that this exists. Large corporations have dominated the use of the research credit. 549 corporations with receipts of $1 billion or more claim over half of the $6 billion of net credit (Highlights of GAO-10-136, a report to Committee on Finance, U.S. Senate). The CEO of any size company can justify costs of development by taking the R&D Credit.

The table below shows examples of big, well known tech and software companies' savings through the tax credit for the 1st quarter of 2013:

Company	Estimated Tax Benefit (in millions)
Google	$380.0
Intel	$290.0
EMC	$75.3
Adobe Systems	$12.9
Yahoo	$9.0
Teradata	$4.0

Thurm, Scott. The Wall Street Journal."The Big Profits: A Research Tax Break." June14, 2013.

To review the article go to: http://online.wsj.com/behindthebigprofits:aresearchtaxbreak

OK, this great for the big guys, but what about smaller companies? There isn't a reason not to investigate the tax credit for a company even if it is small. There is a whole chapter on this later in the book. A great write up on this subject can be found at *Business Week's* article: *The R&D Tax Credit Explained for Small Business.* Here is an excerpt:

> "What kinds of companies should investigate the R&D credit?
>
> Tech companies, software developers, software-as-a-service companies, biotechnology companies, and anyone providing cloud-based technology or services."
>
> Klien, Karen. BusinessWeek. "The R&D Tax Credit Explained for Small Business." August 16, 2011.

To review the article go to: http://www.businessweek.com/small-business/ther&dtaxcreditexplainedforsmallbusiness

These credits are available in the United States and most developed nations in the world. You don't need to be an accountant...I'm not. There are people to do the work for you. You just need to understand that this is a good thing for your company.

You don't have to be one of these behemoths to get the R&D tax credit.

The Ultimate Guide to Tax Credits For Tech Companies

Chapter 4

What is the Research and Development Tax Credit?

You're not, most likely, an accountant specialized in R&D Tax Credits and my aim is not to make you one. For the purpose of this book we will look at a bit of detail at the United States Credits. However, keep in mind that individual States and other countries offer their own R&D credits which raises the amount of savings that can drop to the bottom line.

US Congress created the R&D Credit to stimulate businesses to do more research with the passing of the Economic Recovery Tax Act of 1981. It is not a permanent part of the Tax Code (some people are pushing for it to be), however it gets renewed almost continually by Congress. The most recent renewal was under the American Taxpayer Relief Act of 2012, which extended the credits for the 2012, and 2013 tax years.

There are bills introduced all the time to extend the credit beyond 2013 and it is highly probable that it will be extended buoyed by big business. Big companies lobby for the renewal so it is not going away anytime soon.

It is not a grant, it is not economic stimulus or a government sponsored fellowship. It is a tax reduction on qualified expenses.

If you have not taken advantage of this before then you will also be able to take advantage of a 3-year look back study that can actually result in the IRS <u>writing you a check</u>. You can carry forward unutilized credits up to 20 years.

That's it! This is the most you need to know about the history of the R&D Credit.

Chapter 5

How much can we get?

"The avoidance of taxes is the only intellectual pursuit that still carries any reward." - John Maynard Keynes

The general rule of thumb here is that average tax savings is $20,000 - $40,000+ PER YEAR for every $1,000,000 in total company payroll (including contractors) for most companies. However, I have seen it much higher for people developing software through specialized State incentives. Companies that use software in their product or processes may be able to "double up" on State programs.

I run a small Software As A Service (SaaS) company and we identified almost $100,000 in savings the first time we looked at it. And we are not done....R&D Credits will be the way we do business in the future. This is significant to us. It allows us to improve our product and hire more staff. As a small but quickly growing company it is key and the best part of it was that it was not that hard if you know what you are doing.

Maybe you are running a more mature company and want to keep these savings as pure profit. Go ahead! You deserve it because you built something truly innovative and now are in a position to reap the rewards.

Here are some examples of companies that we have worked with using software in their business:

Small Custom Software Development - $ 79,000 in savings
Parts Manufacturer - $1,000,000 in savings
Engineering and Design Firm - $320,000 in savings
Machining Job Shop - $99,000 in savings
Injection Molding Firm - $230,000 in savings
Adhesive Manufacturer - $190,000 in savings
Civil Engineering Firm - $115,000 in savings

Key Points from Chapter 1:

- Increase Cash Flow!
- Current Year Tax Reduction (Current Year)!
- Tax Refund on Prior Years With Interest!
- Carry Forward Un-utilized credits up to 20 years!

It is a great way to generate cash flow for your business needs!

Chapter 6

Why Didn't Your Accountant Tell You About This?

My accountants did not tell me about this. I found out about it doing research on how to save our company money. Remember, I like fast, easy, quick and big savings wins! I leave no stone unturned looking for them.

I started to speak with some Certified Public Accountants (CPAs) about the R&D Credits and some had heard of them but most did not know much about them. I got into a discussion on R&D Credits with a CPA on a flight back from Europe and he said "look the Tax Code is thousands of pages and changes all the time." He went on to make the analogy "it is like medicine, you have general practitioners and specialists. Most company CPAs are general practitioners and this is specialist stuff. CPAs don't practice this stuff and don't study it and so they generally don't speak with their clients about it."

I got it instantly. Most CPAs don't bring it to their clients or boss because either 1) they don't know about it or 2) don't know how to do it.

Does my CPA know anything about this?

I was working with a small software development company on a development project and I told the CEO about the R&D Credits. He, of course, did not know about the credits and asked me to speak with his CPA. We did just that and funny thing, the CPA did not know either. Not a problem, we educated him in the process. Your CPA will certainly be involved in the process of getting the R&D Credits. Fast forward, they got the credit enabling the development house to hire more staff. The CPA was excited about this new service and is going to bring us to meet with his other software clients.

My CPA said we don't qualify?

CPA's are great at general accountants but if they are not specialists in this area and it never hurts to put another set of eyes on it. I don't want to get into too much detail on what qualifies (more on that later) but more companies qualify than you would think. There are many engineering, technical and industry specific expenses that qualify.

Qualification for the credit is not hard to understand. I like to start working with clients by figuring out if they are doing one or all of the following:

- Your company is doing something technical in nature such as tech companies, software development, software-as-a-service (SaaS), biotech companies, and life sciences

- If you have engineers, chemists, technicians, programmers, scientists, or architects etc.
- The work you're doing is creating or improving a product, process, system or service.

I found that most CPA's that don't specialize in R&D should talk with a specialist to make sure that they are looking at the research activity with the right perspectives. CPA's by their nature don't like change or the unknown. A simple prod by the CEO to "go look at it" may be all that is needed.

I think that we already do this?

That is great, but the question is to what extent? The questions to ask your accounts:

- Who did it?
- When did they do it?
- How did they do it?

If they can't answer you with authority or put a big report on your desk and can't speak to it then you need to take another look at it.

I don't want to get too technical here, but if it was done through estimating and does not qualify and quantify the qualified research expenditures then you may be leaving money on the table. If you did it in the past there may be subsequent years where you can still take advantage. The R&D credits have been around since 1981 and if you missed a year or did not do enough of a detailed study then you should investigate further savings.

Key Points

- Most CPAs are not specialists in R&D Credits
- Your CPA may not even know this exists
- It's your job to ensure that it was done correctly
- You need to push this if you want the savings

Chapter 7

How Do I Know If I Qualify?

Contrary to what some may think you don't need people on staff wearing lab coats and working with test tubes to qualify. If you have engineers, programmers or any other technical people in your company there is a good chance you qualify. It also is the same case if you outsource. All those people doing stuff that you don't understand are probably doing stuff that meets the "test."

If your company is developing new or improved-process, techniques, formula, software or invention that is technical in nature to eliminate uncertainty through the process of experimentation then you may qualify. I know that this is a dense definition so let me boil it down to jargon that is more likely what is talked about in your meetings.

Use the following as a checklist. If you are doing at least one of these things on the list then you absolutely need to check out the R&D Credits. Are you doing any of the following?

- Manufacturing
- Testing

- Fabricating
- Engineering
- Developing New Concepts or Technologies
- Design – Layout, Schematics, AutoCAD
- Prototyping or Modeling
- Testing / Quality Assurance: ISO, UL, Sigma Six, etc.
- Integrating of new machinery (CNC, SLA, SLE, etc.) into existing process
- Developing or improving software
- Automating or streamlining internal processes
- Developing tools, molds, dies
- Developing or applying for patents
- Certification testing
- Developing of new technology
- Trying new materials
- Adding new equipment
- Environmental testing
- Developing or improving production / manufacturing processes
- Developing, implementing or upgrading systems and / or software
- Developing production control software
- Improving or building new manufacturing facilities
- Automating internal processes

- Paying outside consultants / contractors to do any of the above stated activities

All these things may incorporate software and could apply to your business. So, how many of these things are you doing? You probably have at least one and most likely more than that.
What are the industries that qualify?

This book is about R&D Credits for Software. Virtually any company in any industry that is doing at least one of the activities in the previous section should investigate the R&D Credit.

As a Tech CEO, I want to focus on the aspect of software in research and design (although I am more than happy to speak with anyone from any industry). Take a look at the next list as the type of industries that use software as their product or in the manufacturing of their products or delivery of their service.

- Aerospace
- Agriculture
- Apparel & Textiles
- Chemical
- Civil Engineering
- Construction
- Electrical Engineering
- Gaming
- Consumer Goods

- Foundries
- Furniture
- Job Shops
- Laboratories
- Manufacturing
- Mechanical Engineering
- Medical Devices
- Oil & Gas
- Product Development
- Semiconductor
- Software
- System Controls
- Telecommunications

This is not an exhaustive list, but I am sure that you get the idea. In the concept, design, production and delivery of a product or service there is almost always the use of software.

Key Points:

You are probably doing something that should be investigated

Any industry is a good candidate

Concept, design, production and delivery are an indicator of the right activity.

Chapter 8

Are We Too Small To Take Advantage Of This?

It's true that the country's largest corporations take advantage of credits like these....taking advantage of stuff like this is how they get big. Most small and medium sized businesses don't know about this or it is too confusing for them to take advantage. Billions of dollars are at play and small and medium sized companies can take advantage. We have worked with small companies with less than 10 people. The rule of thumb is if the company is technical in nature it should investigate the R&D credit.

Big companies go after these credits but the vast majority of small and medium sized businesses don't. Guidance by the US Government has relaxed some of the R&D Tax Credit regulations qualifications, suggesting that more companies are eligible than previously thought. Activities that qualify are much broader than most people think which makes this a great bottom line strategy for many small and medium sized businesses. Companies performing qualified activities with total

U.S. payroll for staff and contractors over $500,000 may qualify, less if you are a software development company or your product is software.

The regulations were changed to be in harmony with the intent of Congress and are much more taxpayer friendly. They reflect a profound change in the position of the IRS. The regulations:

1. Make it easier for a broader array of companies to qualify their activities as R&D
2. Provide greater flexibility in certain record keeping requirements
3. Significantly expand the definition of internal-use software characteristics

The question if you're a good candidate for doing this is relative. I'll explain in a moment. First, let me state this is where a CEO or a C-Suite person's perspective is important. I advise my clients all the time on the prospective ROI of this activity and help them make the decision to pursue the R&D Credits.

Maybe the best decision is to do nothing now but put in a recording system to capture the R&D expenditures in a year or two to maximize your tax management strategies moving forward.

The relative nature of the question has to do with how your company operates. Let's assume that you are doing the right activity and are in an industry that I have listed in the previous chapter. If you passed that "test" then you need to look at the amount of your expenses dedicated to the qualifying activities.

We have worked with small engineering and design firms that were made up of mostly engineers. On the surface, their payroll was not that high and they were quite small. However, almost everything that they did was directly related to development of product through commercialization. R & D Credits made a lot of sense for them because the majority of their expenses were in R & D.

On the contrary, I consulted with a large manufacturing company that employed engineers but they were manufacturing engineers not contributing enhancements to their product or process. The role of the manufacturer was to take orders and use their customer's specs and formulations to produce private label goods. It is a private label operation based on old technology. The R & D Credits did not make sense for them because although they could get something it was not worth their time.

Bottom line: you can't judge a book by its cover. You need to look at the detail and decide what is right for you.

Key Points:

- Need to look at the activities that your staff is doing
- If you have technical people you're a good candidate
- Perspective of an experienced person will help you decide

Chapter 9

What Is The Right Process To Take The R & D Credits?

There are hard ways and an easy way to do this. There a generally three ways to pursue the R & D Credits:

1. Do it alone
2. Give it to your CPA
3. Hire a firm specializing in the R &D credits

Do it alone

Warning! Don't do it this way. If you put someone from your accounting department on this they will not succeed. They will not get it done and if they do fumble to something that they think is complete ….. it won't be.

The Research and Development Tax Credit is a valuable technique for companies to help fund Qualified Research Expenditures to bring product to market or increase sales. However, it is daunting and scary. Section 41 of the Internal Revenue Code and the Audit Technique Guide: Credit for Increasing Research Activity contains almost 15,000 (14,572) words between them. Not to mention the thousands of words in the related definitions, court case precedents and State Research Credits.

Questions need to be answered:

- What are my Qualified Research Expenditures?
- How do we document them?
- Do I use the Regular Research Credit or the Alternative Simplified Credit?
- What will be the benefit or drawback of each?

The phrase "research or experimental expenditures" is a form of art for tax purposes. The term is similar to the term "research and development costs," as used for financial accounting purposes (FASB Accounting Standards Codification Topic 730). It takes a highly skilled and specialized resource to simplify this for you. This is not for your junior accountant to try to figure out.

In Addition, the following 35 States may have the their own rules and regulations that could result in savings:

Arizona	Kansas	North Carolina
Arkansas	Louisiana	North Dakota
California	Maine	Ohio
Colorado	Maryland	Pennsylvania
Connecticut	Massachusetts	Rhode Island
Delaware	Michigan	South Carolina
Georgia	Minnesota	Utah
Hawaii	Montana	Vermont
Idaho	Nebraska	West Virginia

Illinois	New Jersey	Wisconsin
Indiana	New Mexico	Washington
Iowa	New York	

The States have their own rules, requirements and procedures. There will be more research to qualify and more process to navigate. Do yourself a favor and don't try to do it this way!

Give it to your CPA

Giving it to your CPA is a step in the right direction, but remember about the CPA that told me that you really need a specialist. Just like your Junior Accountant, your CPA does not know the ins and outs of finding, documenting, performing an engineering study and securing the credits.

The good news is that they must be involved and are key to the process as a support person. They will be your eyes and ears by contributing and coordinating activity on your end. Others from your staff will need to be involved from payroll and even some of the engineers or programmers that do the work.

Giving this activity to your CPA to do it by themselves will cost you thousands in billable hours while they try to get up to speed and fall short. Take it from me this something that you don't want to do!

Hire a firm specializing in the R & D credits

This is the recommended way to do this. I consult with companies all the time and advise them to find a specialized experienced firm. This is the preferred method with a qualifier.... find a firm that has the perspective of an executive and is not a bunch of accountants dumping information and paperwork in your lap.

You want to find a firm that takes the lead to get this done for you. You're busy and are bombarded with questions all day long. A firm worth hiring will perform an assessment to understand if it makes sense to invest more time to move forward. Early in the process they need to know enough to make a decision if it makes sense for you to pursue the credits. Their recommendation should be based on an CEO's view and not just "chasing the money." The firm's recommendation must be based in experience of doing the studies and getting the credits for their clients.

My Recommended Process

The process that I follow is designed as a go/no-go stage gate process. It is done over the phone or web-conference in most cases. We educate you and your staff along the way and we spend the hours so you don't have to. We have designed our process to minimize the time that you need to be involved. It is not complicated and is broken down to 4 steps:

Step 1: Qualification: Your Time-20 Minutes

Interview to determine eligibility. This is the step where questions will be asked about your product, staff and process. We can determine if it makes sense to carry forward. Experience will tell us if we want to invest more time into the project that will benefit you. Will you save 10's of thousands or 100's of thousands of dollars or more?

Output: you're qualified with target savings amount

Step 2: Identification: Your Time-1 Hour

Building off of Step 1, we will work with you and your CPA to determine exactly what activities that qualify to be classified as Qualified Research Expenditures (QREs). This gives us a bearing to focus on and what to look at to review. Once we determine these we will ask for some documents like payroll records and job descriptions. We will also speak about your profitability (you don't need to be profitable) to help us determine how we would prepare your study.

Output: education and further definition on key research

That's it! We have enough information to work up some numbers. We do that without you having to have you spend more time with us.

Step 3: Kick-Off: Your Time-30 Minutes

By Step 3 you have invested 1 hour and 20 minutes…. max!. We gathered and discussed your information, looked at your documents and have calculated good numbers that tell you how much we will save you. This is an exciting step for us because we have enough information to tell you if the numbers in Step 1 are even going to be bigger.

Output: more precise numbers

Step 4: Production – 6 Hours

In this step, interviews are conducted with the technical people in your company. People who write code, engineers and others who are involved with producing your product and bringing it to market are debriefed to include their activity into the study.

When all information is gathered our people will perform the required calculations to determine the amount of money that you can use to request a refund, use as a tax credit now and set up your tax planning for the future. The calculations will be used by your CPA to file the necessary tax forms that we prepare.

Perhaps the most important deliverable that you will receive is a detailed Engineering Report that will substantiate the "numbers". These reports can be hundreds of pages of details and records, which are the basis and proof behind the numbers. IRS approved methods to determine the qualifying expenditures in a quantitative manner are used.

Output: detailed engineering report (IRS preferred method) and tax forms

Now What?

You have invested a little time and now you can reap the rewards of the work that was done for you. Your CPA has all the information that he needs to get the tax credit and file for the refund. What are you going to do with the money? Re-invest in the business, take that needed vacation or move to the next generation of the software.

Our Process is an easy 4-step process with 6 to 8 hours total of client time. It's that easy! Where else can you invest that amount of time to get a payback of tens or hundreds of thousands or even millions of hard earned money?

Let's look at some examples of ROI:

$98K credit/8 hours invested = $12,250/hour

$400K credit and return/8 hours invested = $50,000 / hour

$123K credit/ 7 hours invested = $17,571 / hour

$1,200K credit and return/ 8 hours invested = $150,000 / hour

These are great examples of payback on time invested anyway you look at it. And the effort does not have to end after one time. As long as there is an R&D Tax Credit you will be able to claim the credit.

Record keeping-we do that

Here is a little secret .... you will get better at the process each time. The first time that you claim the credit there will be record keeping that will have to be re-created, but as you learn or more importantly as your company learns, you will build these into your process for the future.

I guarantee the first time that you do this that you will not have all the records that you need. No worries! As part of the process the records can be re-created and gathered from all the emails, project plans and payroll receipts that you have. The best thing is that we will teach your staff how to do this so next time it even gets easier.

How Long Will This Take?

This is not as hard as it may seem if you have the right partner. I like to tell people that it 4-8-8 Process. 4 steps in 8 hours to 8 weeks for refund.

<u>4 Steps</u> – Qualification, Identification, Kick-Off and Production

<u>8 Hours</u> – 20 Minutes, 1 Hour, 30 Minutes, 6 Hours

<u>8 Weeks</u> - to refund

4-Steps	8 Hours	8 Weeks
Qualification	20 Minutes	Refund
Identification	1 Hour	
Kick-Off	30 Minutes	
Production	6 Hours	

Sure this is based on averages and some take a little longer and some are done a little quicker. The important thing is that it gets done.

Chapter 10

How Much Does The Research and Design Study Cost?

Nothing up front.....read on! Our process is designed to minimize time and we perform an upfront analysis to determine if we should accept you as a client. As we work the 4-8-8 Process we are building valuable insight to your company.

At the Kick-Off step we are able to present you with the numbers that we will save you. At that point we are 100% confident that we will be able to produce an Engineering Study that will act as the foundation and basis of the qualified research expenditures to get the hundreds of thousands of dollars that are there for you.

If we perform and produce savings through Research and Design Tax Credits we will invoice you in the form of a performance contract. The performance contract allows us to conduct the study and give you an IRS accepted R&D Engineering Study just the way they like to see it.

If we don't find that you are a good candidate for the study then you owe us nothing!

Chapter 11

How To Get Started?

Congratulations, you made it this far in the book and you are on your way to get the money that will help you grow your business.

I can write another 100 pages on things like record keeping, qualified research expenditures and time value of money…but I won't. The reason that I won't is because I wrote this book to give you the knowledge of what R&D Tax Credits are and a little about how they work. My aim was nothing more than to get you to this point to know that this is something that you need to act on.

Big companies like Google, Intel and Apple use this tax strategy each and every year to save billions of dollars. The difference between them and you is that they have huge teams of tax attorneys, specialists and consultants to help them navigate this complex subject. As a CEO of a Software Company, I know that you have a lot on your plate and this most likely is not in your wheelhouse. I found out about this and acted on it and returned some of our own hard earned money to my company to fund more development. I can help you do the same.

As I mentioned earlier in the book, I love to chase down savings and I felt so strongly that I could help other tech and software companies do this that I developed a company to do just that. I am driven to help other people and I know I can help you make the right decision for your company.

But are you eligible for our "coding your tax credit" consultation?

What I want you to do right now is to go to www.taxcreditsfortechcompanies.com and fill in your information. We will be in touch to schedule your free consultation. In less than 20 minutes, we will be able to tell you if we can accept you into our program.

Chapter 12

Final Thoughts

Being a CEO of a Software or Tech company is hard and that is why there are not that many of us. You got into the business because you wanted to fill a need or just produce a great product. You probably are a small or medium sized company that got funding through your own savings, credit cards, friends & family, angel investors or even maybe venture capital. There is always someone to answer to whether it is your partner, spouse, bank or your investors.

I get it, sometimes it is hard to focus on the business side of your company when all you want to do is follow your vision to change the world with your software. Maybe you measure yourself by growing sales or your user base. In 100% of every software company that I know you need money and likely more of it to achieve what drives you.

Most of you probably hate to look at the balance sheet or cash flows. This is not what drives you, but you do know that you need money to hire developers, get space and acquire users. Your bank, spouse or investors want to know how you are going to do it. Your spot is lonely at times; no one feels the pressure that you do. Not your CFO, COO or Board. You must produce results to keep this whole thing on the tracks.

If someone told you that they were going to drop a few hundred thousand dollars in your lap, what would you do with it? You probably would dream about growing your business, developing that new kick ass feature or launching that "other" thing that you wanted to do for so long.

I am offering just that….a way to do the things that you want to do by dropping money in your lap. No one can start the ball rolling but you. You're the one in charge. The one that now has the answer how to keep growing.

I am one of you, The Software CEO, who works just like you. I stumbled on some information about R&D Tax Credits and got them the hard way. I am offering you a chance to work with someone that is just like you to do this for you and all you have to do is take the first step!

Chapter 13

About The Author

Entrepreneur, business owner, CEO, executive management - Joe has done them all. He has launched and sold businesses, brought new products & services to market and turned around struggling businesses.

He has been featured in blogs, written articles, seen in international newspaper articles & has spoken at conferences and executive management courses. He continues to guest blog, speak and share his message on growing profitable businesses.

When Joe is not working on an idea or with a company, he loves to be outdoors and travel internationally with his family.

If you're interested in speaking with Joe contact him at: joeskulski@element56.com

Share Your Opinion!
Please Leave A Review on Amazon

Thank you so much for becoming a trusted reader of **The Ultimate Guide To Tax Credits For Tech Companies**.

Please take a few moments to log into amazon.com and write a quick review, this will be of great service to me and help me to write you even better books going forward.

Note -- Here is a definition of the ranking system:

- ★☆☆☆☆ I completely let you down.
- ★★☆☆☆ There were problems with my service.
- ★★★☆☆ I could have done better.
- ★★★★☆ My services met your expectations.
- ★★★★★ **You enjoyed and learned much from reading this book.**

www.ingramcontent.com/pod-product-compliance
Lightning Source LLC
Chambersburg PA
CBHW040816200526
45159CB00024B/3003